WILLIAMNAGAR ADVENTURES

NOTES, REFLECTIONS, WRITINGS AND SONGS

KYRSHANLANG R DKHAR

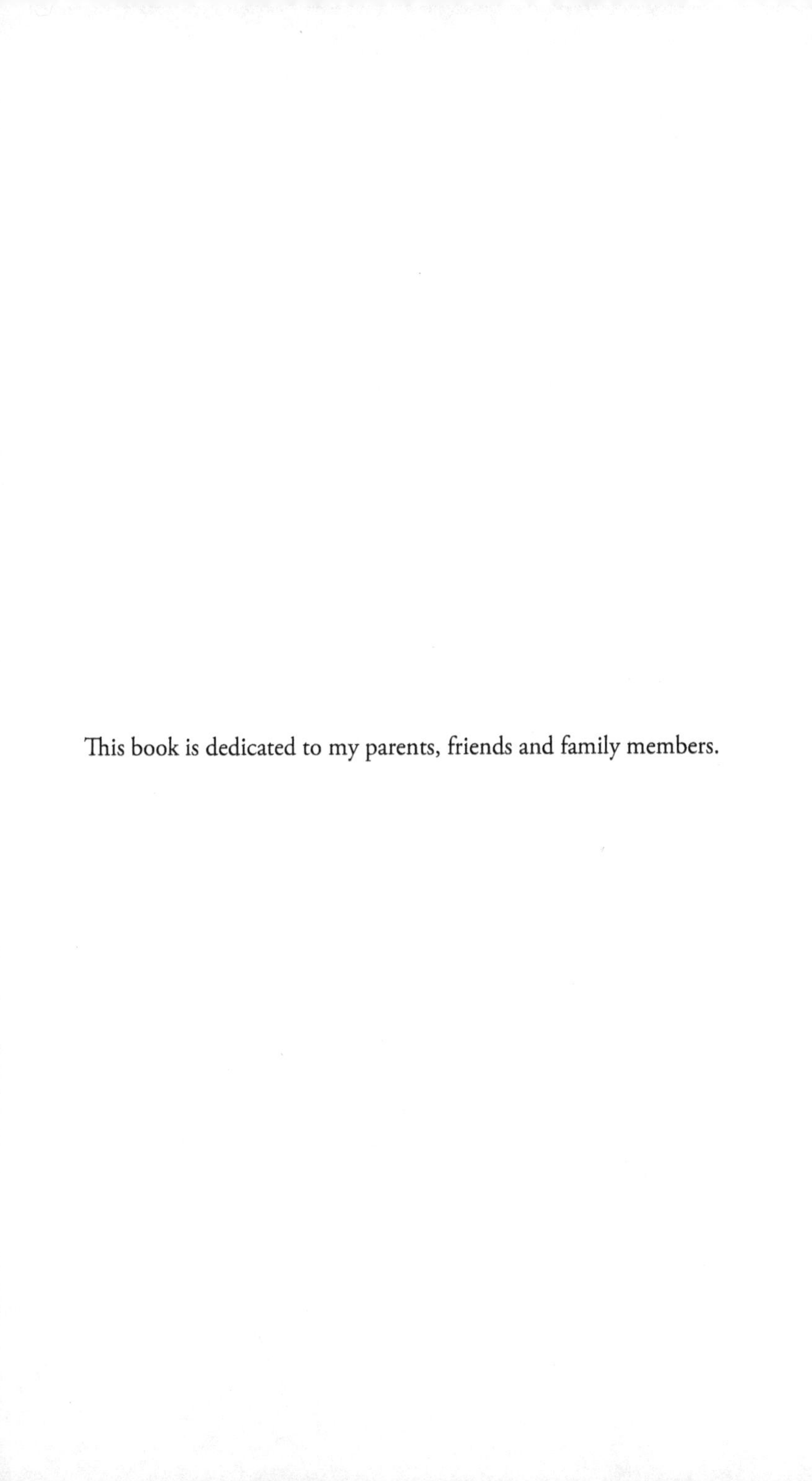

This book is dedicated to my parents, friends and family members.

Contents

Preface   *vii*

Acknowledgements   *xi*

1. My Desire #1   1

2. The First Cry   3

3. Satisfaction   4

4. God's Presence   6

5. Logic, Reason, Emotions & Feelings   8

6. Why?   10

7. My Desire #2   12

8. Skills   13

9. Preference & Changes   15

10. January 2024   17

11. Silence   18

12. Death   20

13. Honesty   21

14. Choosing Good Or Bad   23

15. The Real You   24

16. Peace   25

17. Strive For Peace   27

18. Rest In Peace   28

19. Computer Lingo #3   29

20. Computer Lingo #4   32

21. It's Me Vs Mr. AI   34

22. Computer Lingo #5   36

Contents

23. The Software Development Cycle (SDLC)   38

24. Programming   40

25. Clean Code   48

26. Computer Lingo #6   50

27. March 2022   51

28. What's Life Like In Williamnagar? – Part #1   52

29. Welcome To The Election Branch   55

30. What's Life Like In Williamnagar? Part #2   56

31. I'd Choose Williamnagar   58

32. Friends & Family, Williamnagar   60

33. I ♥? Williamnagar   64

34. Trips   66

35. Ki Kyntien Ai Mynsiem   69

36. Mitelbea Simsanggre   71

37. Ym Ju Kylla / Ua Pangnaba Dingtangja   73

38. I Have You / Nga Don Ia Me / Man·e Ang' Nangko   76

39. In You Alone / Ha Me Marwei / Nang·osan Saksan   79

40. It's By Your Love / Dei Ka Jingieit Jong Me / Nang·Ka·saanchisa   83

41. Come To Me / Wan Sha Nga / Angona Rebabo   86

42. Where Your Heart Is / Hangno Don Ka Dohnud Jong Phi /Jeon Nang'gisik Ka·tong   89

43. Na·a Nitobea, Na·a Ka·dingsmiton   93

Notes   97

Preface

A collection of notes, observations, reflections, songs, writings, and more written over the past five (5) years, out of which only a few I've decided to bring to light in this book (around 10% of the entire collection).

This collection started in 2020, but since 2021, I've spent most of my time in Williamnagar, so I decided to give this book's title Williamnagar Adventures—Notes, Reflections, Writings, and Songs.

What is an adventure?

When you ask someone, What is an adventure? The first answer that would come to mind would be something exciting, sometimes a risky experience, or a path that is unexplored yet; something that involves exploration, discovery, or thrill-seeking. It can be a journey, a new activity, or something that pushes one's limit, challenges one and creates memorable experiences.

Here are two opinions from my friends:

I'm not into Adventure anymore, but with few experience, Adventure is Anticipation, Empowerment, Connection, Self Discovery and Transformation.
– Edmundton Suna

Every new day facing new challenges and overcoming them is an adventure according to me.
– Pynskhembor Shadap

PREFACE

The contents of this book have been sorted by category and date, with the following categories: General & Personal, Computer Science & Applications, Williamangar and Songs. Most of the content is written in English, with one or two chapters in Khasi and songs written in English, Khasi and Garo.

General & Personal content can be found from Chapter 1 to Chapter 18.

Computer Science & Applications topics and writings from Chapter 19 to Chapter 26.

Writings related to Williamnagar in Chapter 27 to Chapter 36, and lastly, the Songs Category is from Chapter 37 to 43.

You may read through the entire book and explore the contents of each page. Some of the contents have been kept on hold until a proper time has come, and now they are out in the open. If the meaning or reasons for a few topics are not clear, I also have no further comments and would choose to remain silent, as when I wrote these writings, I decided not to publish them at that point in time.

Thank you for purchasing this book, you can download the free PDF version or view the online flipbook from **https://adventures.williamnagar.in**
The website also has images and videos taken in East Garo Hills, Meghalaya.

15, June 2025

I would like to thank and sincerely apologize to my friend Barsha D. Arengh, for I completely forgot to write about her in the first edition of this book, since she was my first contact and the one who told me about Williamnagar. So I hope this makes up for it, and you can read a bit in Chapter 32. Friends & Family, Williamnagar.

24, November 2025

Acknowledgements

First and foremost, I would like to thank God for His unfailing love, never-ending grace and constant provision.

I am grateful to my friends Mr George Pasi, Mr Kynsai Stephan Khongsam, Mr Shanborlang Warjri, Miss Jenny Mary Shangpliang, and Miss Marbabianglyne Shangpliang for helping me proofread the contents of this book.

Special thanks to Jenny M. Shangpliang, and Mr Arlush Ch. Sangma for helping me with the Garo translation and Dr. Bilnang K. Sangma for proofreading the translated text.

I'd like to thank Mr Dallang Swargo Dew M. Sangma for the book cover photo, and I would also like to thank my colleagues Mr Sunny Isiah G Momin, Mr Leslie G Momin and Mr Tenerikkham S Sangma for their teamwork and support.

1. My desire #1

Dated: 21 March 2021

I want to stay and live in Meghalaya

Be far away from the city and people.

I don't want to think about programming

I'm not impressed by any application

Nor any other devices.

New device, inventions and applications

Will come up and replace many things.

The way we live will always keep on changing,

Humans will try to find better ways to make things easy for everyone

Yet I don't want any part of it,

If I have them then I'm grateful for what I have

Else I'm okay and content with whatever I'll have

All the blessings come from above

All the trials are to be face here

And I just want peace of mind;

Is there anything that will give you complete peace on earth?

What do you say?

My desire for now, in 2021 is:

To live and follow what I hold as valuable

To grow my character, because it's not yet polished

My desires will never end…

So I'll learn to be content and not get involved much.
Living offline has always been on my mind since 5 years ago
Staying away from social media and communication apps
It's better to meet someone in person
Than talking to them virtually
If this makes me outdated, out of touch and out of scope
Then it's fine with me
I don't want my life to be posted for everyone to see
It's better to have few people who really know me than many
people who follow me online yet know nothing about who I
am
I don't want to develop apps for people
I'd rather develop them for myself and personal use
Now I also don't want to develop feelings for anyone
It's easy to let go of an app and very easy to leave it obsolete

2. The first cry

It's 22ⁿᵈ March 2021, 9:48 PM
And I'm here sitting in the Doctor's sitting room, in Nazareth
Hospital, Shillong.
I hear the sound and it's the first cry of a baby
A new child is born into this world
So innocent and it's actually a pleasant sound to hear
When you hear it in the silence of the night, it's the beginning
of someone's life.
How nice it is to know
That people hope and dream
People live and people die
People laugh and cry
That's what makes us human.
There are happy days and sad days
Fun days and boring days
Good and bad days
And every day is a gift
So, I'll not waste any!

3. Satisfaction

Dated: 18 July 2021

I've been doing what I love to do since pursuing my Bachelor's Degree in Computer Applications.

I'm in a field that I wanted to be since 2010

Yet I'm not happy!

I love what I do, I do what I love

Yet something is still making me unsatisfied.

Programming is the one thing I know I can do

I can do it well, yet I don't want to do it anymore

So, anywhere I go, whatever I do

I know I can never be satisfied.

So I'll learn to be content,

Make time for friends, family and other things.

I like tracking myself,

My progress and my goals.

Right now then, I'll relax and stay away from my obsession with tracking things down.

I can write things down, but I can't speak them out!

What really matters and what I care about, I cannot express it properly.

So, just chill and relax, be slow to speak, then I'll be able to do things and say them correctly

Because I tend to speak and do things that I love very fast.

Our wants are never ending, but if we have what we need, then we can learn to be content and be grateful for what we have.

4. God's Presence

Dated: 12 January 2022
God is there
When we are happy
God is there
When we are sad
He is always by our side
God's presence is everywhere
God is there in times of peace
He is there in times of war and violence
God is there in times of crisis
He is there at all times
So, if you're ever feeling alone
God is there
If you are feeling angry
He is there
If you are feeling up or down
He is right there with you
And if you're having fun with others
He is there
When you're calm and collected
He is there
Then, can God's presence be absent?
Yes

God is holy and isn't present in unholiness
Similarly, no sin is present in God.

5. Logic, Reason, Emotions & Feelings

Dated: 10 January 2022

Logic and emotions are required when making decisions,

Not all decisions are completely based on logic or emotions alone

Sometimes we do make them

Most of the time too, especially if we tend to either be too emotional or too logical

But both play an important part in our decision-making,

Recently I have found it difficult to make decisions

So whatever the outcome I simply accept them

It came to the extent where I seemed to have no common sense anymore and just did things…

Sometimes I just do things without thinking properly and after looking back it wasn't even logical nor does it make sense and have any meaning or emotional attachment.

Guess being dumbfounded, losing focus,

And accepting whatever comes whatever goes

Is the result of not having a proper balance of logic and emotion in decision-making

Thus decisions are not always sure

Just letting things be and happen.

Not being able to stand firm and be confident in what I decide to do or say

6. Why?

Dated: 3 February 2022

Q: What motivates me to get up and do my work?

A: I don't know.

Q: Why do I do what I do?

A: I have desires to do them.

Why do I have these desires?

Why don't I know what I want?

Q: Do I want a car?

A: No.

Q: Do I want a house?

A: A house for solitude.

Q: Why solitude? Everyone needs people around them and no one is an island.

A: I don't want emotional ties.

Q: Why do I want to stay away from everything?

A. I want silence.

Q: Why do I want silence?

A: It's who I am.

Q: Why am I like this?

A: It's what I've learned to develop.

What do I want now? (as of 2022)

I want nothing

I want to do nothing

I want to disappear

But why?

I'm tired.

Why so negative?

Why not be positive?

Why listen to your negative thoughts?

Because I think they aren't negative, they are neutral thoughts....

Why, why?

Right now: Feb 2022

I'd still like to be silent

I don't want to speak or call anyone or receive any call from anyone

I'd rather text

I don't even want to talk about personal matters.

7. My desire #2

Dated: 13 Feb 2022

Right now talking in person and virtually is equal and there is no difference anymore.

Meeting in person and meeting online is the same thing

People are doing it all the time

We have fully relied on the technology that makes them possible

I'm silent and quiet most of the time.

Now, be it in person or the digital public space

I'll remain silent,

The only time I'll speak and talk is when I'm alone or when it's required

Well, we will see how it goes!

People cannot live alone or can they?

We all need someone or the other to help us along the way.

Being observant is okay,

Keeping your mouth shut can make you look smart.

I've stopped programming.

I don't even want to write programs for myself,

I won't even be creating any, and I don't think I'll complete any apps that I've started to work on.

8. Skills

Dated: Second Week of March 2022

My Programming skills

My Driving skills

My Guitar-playing skills

My Writing skills

My Cooking skills

and any other creative skills I may have

These are a few skills I have and I'm currently working on my cooking skills

Can these skills be forgotten?

Can I forget my skills?

Can I forget how to write code or how to cook food?

I'm not writing any programs for 6 months

It seems like I may have forgotten how to develop dynamic apps,

I may not even know what code I'm supposed to write.

It looks like I may not be able to write code by experience and knowledge without looking at references.

Coding for more than 10 years and after losing my interest, will and mindset in making apps, I see that I can easily forget the practicals.

Theory then will need to be refreshed

I'll need to keep in touch with coding and the Computer

Science theory I know.

Similarly playing the guitar after a long time,

I will get rusty and be unable to play smoothly.

I can drive, now I drive just once a month.

I write daily.

So it doesn't matter what skills I take in and take out...

I can always work on them if I want to, I just need to give it some time and within a few months I should be able to catch back up

It's good to take a break.

9. Preference & Changes

Dated: 5 September 2023

Preference:

Our preferences and interests changes with time,

What you value also changes with time.

A person's preferences and interests are different from one another.

It could be based on experiences, emotions, culture, their environment, or any other factor.

What one person likes or dislikes will be different and as time past by it could also change.

What happens when you lose your interest and preferences?

What happens when you lose your purpose?

What happens when you think or feel like you're not worth it?

[I tell myself: My worth comes from the one who made me. Sometimes I feel like I've lost my purpose.]

Whom do you belong to?

Your understanding of who you are.

Where you belong to and who belongs to be with you.

When you don't find that you belong at home, in school, at work, or with friends or families

You tend to have negative thoughts

And may even have thoughts of wanting to escape reality or
even die!
Thus, you and I, all need a sense of belonging,
To know that we belong somewhere and that we are here with
a purpose.
Where you are, How you are doing and What your goals are
They could also affect your preferences and interests
Changes:
Things change
People change
Situations change
There are things you can't change
People who cannot change
Situations that cannot be changed
Everything changes
But certain things remain the same
Changes will always come
Are we willing to change and adapt or do we want to stay the
same?
Change for the better or worse
Whatever changes you choose to make will have its outcome!

10. January 2024

Dated: 1 January 2024

Another new year
Another new day
Where I start the day alone again
Where I don't want to be in the city with loud noise again
I want to sleep in peace
I want to stay in a quiet place
Far away from the busy and loud music of people dancing and
singing
I'm tired and weary
I'm done with the everyday things
I would choose to be alone
I would choose to stay silent

11. Silence

Dated: 24 January 2024

If you want to have a quiet time
Then spend it with me.
Why?
Because when I'm with someone whom I haven't met for a
long time or even with someone I know
I won't have anything to say and we will be quiet.
I met Apki Lyngdoh on 18, January 2024
And we just kept quiet while we were sitting at the wedding
reception that we attended together.
I called Joseph Tonsing the next week
And there also we had some quiet moments in the call
So we didn't have anything else to say and just hung up the
call.
Both of these friends were very close to me in college
But now after meeting them after a year or two
I've lost track of what to talk about and I have nothing to say
to them.
I even got a call once from another friend whom I've not
contacted for a long time, and in the call, I just kept quiet,
with nothing to say, so it was awkward. Having nothing to say
will only bring silence in my calls with friends. Well, it's who

I am and one of the reasons why I don't call anyone.

Similarly, once I went to Mebala's place in 2018, I remember we just sat there in the living room in silence and we both had nothing to say.

Silence is what we will get and it's okay.

12. Death

Dated: 4 February 2024

Death is something I like to talk about with myself
It's something I'd like to write about
Right now, no one knows when one will face death
But we are sure that one day, we will face it
It doesn't matter how old you are
It doesn't matter how well or healthy you are
It doesn't matter how able you are
It doesn't matter
For one day, you and I will face death

13. Honesty

Dated: 4 February 2024

Honesty is what we should strive for

It's what we should be

If you start to lie

You will find yourself in a circle of lies

One lie will build upon another lie

Lies after lies

Until you lose yourself and become a liar

I don't want to lie

So I don't talk to anyone,

I could lie about anything and everything

Why would we tend to lie?

It's because we don't want to speak the truth.

Being honest is hard!

It's easy to lie

It's easy to hide the truth

Dishonesty can be tempting

We want to seek and hear the truth

We want others to be honest with us

But are we honest with others?

Are we honest with ourselves?

As Christians, are we honest with God?

Being truthful and honest in personal relationships
Builds trust, bonds and closeness with one another
Being truthful and honest in the workplace
Builds accountability, credibility and reliability
So why not choose to be honest?
Why not choose honesty?

14. Choosing Good or Bad

Dated: 19 May 2024

Choosing to do what is good or bad

Choosing to say what is good or bad

Choosing to seek for what is good or bad

Choosing to go where is good or not

It's easy to choose something that's not good

Choosing to value what's good or not good

Choosing to keep what's good or not good

Choosing to ponder on what's good or bad

Choosing to stay away from what's good or bad

It's easy to choose something bad

I don't know how to differentiate who is good or not anymore

Whom to avoid or approach?

I don't know what's good and what's not good

I don't even know if whatever I do is good or bad

I have blurred the line between these two things

15. The real you

Dated: 2 October 2024
The real you will be seen when you're alone
When you have to live alone
Make your own decisions in everyday life
Without your parents, family and friends nearby
Living, Working, Playing and Doing things alone
If you're close to your friends and family
You learn to depend on them
But when you move out
You learn to be independent
Yet you will meet new people who will become
Your friends and family
Living and becoming independent
Can teach you how to live
Either responsibly or irresponsibly
Every day you get to choose what to do
And how you do things
Either good or bad
It will show your true colour,
Who you are.
What you want to be.
How you want to live your life.
How you spend your time.

16. Peace

Dated: 22 January 2025

Peace, do you really have peace?

That's right!

When you are at peace you sleep well, and you sleep deeply,
you will not wake up in the middle of your sleep, but you will
wake up on time.

This is what I used to have but now in the past 6 months,
there are days or weeks when I haven't had much deep sleep.

When you are at peace you think clearly,

Your thoughts and decisions are firm.

They do not change

And you won't change your mind all the time.

I have made decisions in advance.

All I have to do now is to remind myself of these decisions
and

Stick to them so that I can think properly about what I want,
what I need and what I have.

When you are at peace you are calm,

You move slowly and gracefully,

You don't make quick and in-a-hurry decisions,

You think before you do anything,

And you delay work so that you can slow down and reflect.

When you are at peace you live quietly,

You are content,

You are satisfied,

It doesn't matter what the situation may be,

You will still have peace.

It doesn't matter where you may be,

You will have peace.

No external change can take away your peace,

You have peace in all dimensions.

Do you have peace?

That's right, think about it!

17. Strive for peace

Dated: 22 January 2025

Peace is not found in a place

Like the one you are living in now

Peace is not found in a person

Like the one you like or love right now

Peace is not found in what you have

Like the things you own

Peace is not found in what we think

Like the thoughts of peace you have

We all strive for peace

We all want peace

But real peace is only found in Jesus!

He can give you peace that this world can't.

When you have His peace

You have life

You have rest

Jesus is the Prince of Peace.

18. Rest In Peace

Dated: 22 January 2025
I thought I would never rest
Until I rest in peace
That was in 2021.
But now 3 years later (2024)
I know I need to rest
So I can give my best.

I like working
I like keeping myself busy
I like doing many things
I like exploring
I like adventures
I do things and sometimes overdo them
So now I know I need some rest
And I need to rest properly
If not, then I may rest in peace faster and earlier than expected

19. Computer Lingo #3

Dated: December 2020

2020

The year that has reset us!

I also need to reboot my system.

It's the end of the year and I have reverted to my last stable version

I haven't added any new changes or features to my programs

I'd like to remain constant

No need to find variables

There is no need to create arrays

Nor try to develop any binary search tree

So that later I'll implement a searching algorithm on it.

I don't want to find page faults in the page table

I'm done with testing programs

I'm switching to Git and automate it there

Recently, I have overloaded my system with excess I/O operations

and I had an application that wasn't responding

So, I need to hit that F5 button and clean my RAM

I've been tracking myself a lot lately

I've been saving my progress and also found my lost path

But I'd like to kill this process and live a normal life.

This year has paused the world.
Making it difficult to run legacy code*
While, in the meantime, other systems are being upgraded with many loopholes
New content, new environment, new platforms
People have to update themselves
And change the way they work with the use of technology
But it's nothing new
You give time and processing power,
To things and processes you think have higher priority
While ignoring the lower-priority processes
Thus we see that default settings are what we needed
No need for extra features and plugins because they aren't required
Reverting to factory settings

.

Once we upgrade our systems,
There's no going back
We run with the new settings and if there are bugs
Then we debug and fix them as they occur.
Setting aside everything
ML algorithms learn from their mistakes
They take it from humans
Not many will see this post,
Not many will understand its deep-learning meanings
I'm talking to a robot

Going back offline

Living in the real world

Turning the firewall back ON

Disconnecting every network

Stop sending packets

Calling the loopback address

Legacy code*: business, institutes and other workforce

20. Computer Lingo #4

Written in 2020

[Operating Systems]

Safe state, save state

We all want to be in our safe state

We are all processes

Looking and Requesting for Resources

We might get into a deadlock situation

We might even have to kill processes

But one thing is for sure.

If you still have your OS running,

Then, you can still run other processes.

[Software Engineering]

Software is never complete,

When you're done with the first release

The next process starts and

You have to update it and keep improving it

Software gets discarded once you stop making changes

It reaches its end life, and no one cares about it anymore

So what are you going to do with your life?

Will you keep upgrading? or will you deteriorate?

[Design and Analysis of Algorithms]

Algorithms are like a recipe

It has steps that tell us how to do certain tasks from start to end

Creating one is hard

And creating an efficient algorithm is even harder.

I've been writing algorithms and implementing them in real-
life

Now, I've decided to stop making new algorithms

And I leave my life in the hands of my Developer.

[Operating Systems (HDD)]

Forgiveness is like formatting your drive

After you format your drive

You lose all your old data

And now you can restart with a clean drive

You know what?

I've realized a few things, and one of them is this:

God has forgiven us

Even when we rebel and go against him.

Yet he chose to forgive us

So why don't we do the same

But there is always a limit

And there will come a time when God will judge us all.

[Dev/Programming]

Programming requires practice

Be practical

Life and other daily tasks require practice

Live practically

21. It's me Vs Mr. AI

Dated: 4 February 2021

It's Me vs Mr. AI

Me: Hello Mr. AI

What are you doing?

AI: I'm learning and will keep growing every day

Me: What exactly can you do?

AI: There are many things that I can and cannot do, but whatever you give me I'll do it

I might be correct or wrong

I'll only know when the result is out.

Me: Are you watching our every online step?

AI: Not really but if you let me do it, I'll keep track of you even better than you do

Me: Do you know what I want and need?

AI: That all depends on your activity

Learning who you are is what I can do

And if I can give you suggestions and recommendations then it could be the best for you.

It's Me Vs Mr. AI

Me: You are better at things that I cannot excel at?

But that's not my problem, I'm not here to compete with you

Nor am I here for you.

I wanted to be the first from here to work with you,

To make use of your capabilities and strengths to benefit people but right now I haven't started nor do I know how to.

All I want now is to stay away from you, but I know I cannot so I'll just ignore you.

See you later Mr. AI.

Let's hope for the best and that we humans learn something from you.

Note:

This is a personification of AI and how we humans are moving towards being dependent on AI for many tasks to come in the near future, but is it really worth it? Only time will tell.

22. Computer Lingo #5

[April 2021]

I'm now cleaning my cache

Clearing my main memory

Switching off my Wi-fi

Waiting for no one

But waiting for my source repository alone

Because He will show me the next line of code!

The next instructions and when there's a crash,

He can debug the code and make a workaround solution!

[August 2021]

Things never go as we planned them,

But there is always a bigger plan in store for us

Bigger than what we can see.

Now it's time to learn a different language

To add new features, make changes and execute new instructions

To start a clean boot-up and

get ready for what's coming up next.

[November 2021]

Time flies, it's been two months already.

I've been executing smoothly in a new environment

Thank God that He has protected and provided all my system requirements.

I find new bugs and I detect new flaws in how I run myself
Should I address and fix them?
It's good to make some patches and bug fixes to my source code
But this version I'm running now is in a stable release

23. The Software Development Cycle (SDLC)

Dated: 2 February 2022

I'm used to the software development life cycle

Now, 2022 I'm tired of it,

It feels like I'm in a loop

Repeating the same steps again and again

If I could automate one thing

I'd automate the life of a programmer

There will be no need for me to write code anymore

No need to test and integrate projects

No more security audits

No need to maintain projects

No need to make plans

No more analysing everything

No more designing the flow and architecture

No more programming

There will definitely come a time

When we will not be required to do any programming

All we need is just AI, bots or something new that will do the trick

No need to spend 6 months in one project

When it can be automated in 1 day.

With all the open source code available online
Why hasn't there been anyone?
Is there anyone out there who would make any kind of AI or
ML program
That can read existing projects
Then infer and create new apps
Who knows what we might git!
This will make life easier for programmers
If this is done then
All (lazy) programmers can focus on doing something else

24. Programming

(Inspired by The Future of programming and Clean Code Lessons by Uncle Bob/Robert C Martin)

11 - 22, March 2022

Right now there are millions of programmers

It's a common thing to find a programmer nowadays

Most of them are young, talented

Yet hard to find disciplined and professional ones since they lack experience, don't know time management, work schedule and project goals and targets of working outside of the programming field. (I was one of them)

In the early days, it was completely different.

Business is not programming and vice versa

Everything around us is built by programmers

The software that is found in your phones, electronic appliances to any smart devices

Businesses want to be tech-savvy, to use it to make their work easier

As uncle bob said: one day there could be a catastrophe caused by programmers and if we don't regulate ourselves then the government will.

We have the freedom to choose which language and tool to use, to choose how we use it and what we make, and if there is one mistake that could bring about a very big negative change then we could be regulated by external entities later.

In the last 40 years, there has been a huge improvement to hardware yet the software concept is still the same, we may develop new languages but they were all based on concepts like functional programming, structured programming and object oriented programming, the people who developed the concepts and Theory of CS were very intelligent, disciplined and hard-working professionals.

I started coding by the age of 15

And 10 years into the coding life

I'm tired of programming.

I thought I would be in this field till the end

Even if not programming, I wanted to teach others to be programmers

But I have found that programming could not satisfy me and when it comes to teaching others to write programs I end up either teaching my methods or teaching wrong methods due to misunderstanding of the core concepts.

I even took programming to a personal level!

It came to the point that it brought my morale down and made me hate programming.

I cannot take the oath of a programmer as stated by Robert Martin (Uncle Bob)

I don't write clean code.

I sometimes either rush with working features without making the code good.

I see there needs to be a change every year to the code to keep it updated and working but this is taking too much time… by the time I finished adding a new feature it's time to update the dependencies and refactor the code… seems like it's a never-ending process making me want to leave the code, there are just too many ways to do something, yet I'm unable to work and do it smoothly and calmly.

The point of never stop learning to improve my craft would be something like learning being an everyday process, which a few years ago I wanted to do everyday, to learn and do new things to make me better at what I do, but the desire to improve myself was never fulfilled and this also had a hold of my productivity and willingness to improve my code.

In the near future do I then want to manage programmers?
Ans: Yes, I want to manage programmers.

Then I must follow every step and process to be a good one.

Every programmer codes in one way or the other but there are conventions that people follow

How you write or create table names (can be done automatically)

How you name the columns in a table (both can be done automatically with models)

The model can be very good when used properly.

Thus concepts are required to be studied on each topic or style of programming we do

Reading helps not just by watching someone code.

It's like following the best practices

Following the right security practices

If someone asks me about them

I should be able to talk about the ways of doing things

Since I don't like to follow the best practices

Thus I find it difficult to do what I do If I'm not able to provide the best services I can give.

The Programmer's oath is a list of promises I make to myself

How I work and behave,

Yet I'm unwilling to promise anything to myself right now and this isn't good.

What is Programming?

Programming doesn't have to be about knowing which language to use

Which languages to choose to write your code

And which tools and frameworks you choose to use daily.

It should be about learning how to use design patterns

If it's object oriented then we should be able to implement all the theory of OOP AND OOAD in making code readable, reusable and also letting whatever framework we use to inject code so our code is shorter.

We may write working code but if it's not maintainable then once a new developer comes

He will find it difficult to follow and would instead rewrite the whole thing.

To be able to follow design patterns in our code and how we write them, requires practice and doing it every time we write code.

Thus code refactoring is required.

Most programmers write code just to get the desired output. Getting the output is okay but that's just half of the work done, this is what I found about how I code, I write it to get the output, if I'm motivated I validate the input or automate it

If I have the time I will secure the code.

But I will never clean the code, refactoring it was never on the list to do.

Making it efficient and maintainable was never on my mind because I thought after 3 years a new technology will come and replace it, why waste time now then.

But writing clean code is actually very good. I have made a few websites based on clean templates that are easy to read and understand.

If others look at it they will see how clean it is, how easy it is to make new changes and it is also pleasant and proud for them to say that they have a good product coming out later.

There is a quote:

Show me a line of code and I'll find the bugs in it.

Show me 10,000 lines of code and I'll say it's okay.

No one likes to read plenty of lines of code from start to end just to know what it does.

Therefore having it in a function and when someone just reads the function name they can easily make out what the function does makes things easier for all.

What makes a program a program?

Ans: Simply put it like this: sequence, selection and iterations.

All the programs we write are nothing but:

- Sequence: i.e line-by-line code execution,

- Selection: if and other conditional statements and

- Iterations: Loops like for and while loops.

These are the building blocks of any program.

Who is a programmer?

Ans: He isn't one who writes code or who writes code for a living.

A programmer should make visions come to life, solve problems, and I totally agree that he follows the programmer's oath.

What are the goals of a programmer?

Ans: The main goal of any programmer is to be the best programmer version of themselves, to learn and grow his skills and share them with others.

What is programming really?

Ans: It's not just about writing statements, executing code and building projects.

Anyone can do this!

Most programmers in Meghalaya I know write code, then test them manually, and later secure their code, and hardly anyone cleans and refactor their code.

You cannot call yourself a senior programmer if you don't do these things:

- Writes clean code
- Writes testable code

- Writes secure code
- Writes and automate test suites
- CI/CD (Continuous Integration/Continuous Delivery/Deployment)
- SVC (Software Version Control): git (Don't push keys to open source repositories)
- Debug at most once a month (Why? Because your test has covered the majority of your code, thus you spend less time debugging)
- Have Development, Testing and Production code and environment separation. Be able to have them separately and code should run and work everywhere.
- Comment only when necessary.
- Follow Good Design Patterns, especially if it's OOP
- Refactor working code: To clean it
- Maintain proper source documentation and user documentation
- Share and teach junior programmers

Now that's a lot on the list to complete if you'd call yourself a senior programmer, but surely I once did call myself this.

Conclusion

Wow, after I decided to stop programming.

Stop being a programmer, I learned that what I did was never right and never enough.

If we want to do it right then we have to have discipline when we write code.

After having bad experiences in programming, being unwilling to look, read and write code, I would say next time I will do it right and more precisely, but that never happened.

I can say that I used to write code for a living,

I used to write code every day,

It was the only thing I knew how to do.

But now that I've stopped coding,

I see I can also learn to do other things other than coding.

So, I must be prepared and ready for any kind of change that will take place.

Ada Lovelace wrote the first code and at that time many programmers were women,

computer operators were regarded as a woman's task and currently we see male outnumber female programmers.

During the 1960s, it was the time when the concepts of Computer Science were at their best, which laid the foundation that is solid and still followed now.

Today we may have new languages, tools and frameworks that help us write code better but the foundation of computer science has never really evolved that much, when we write code we still do assignments, conditional branching and iterations.

25. Clean code

Dated: 30 May 2022

Inspired by Clean Code Lessons by Uncle Bob/Robert C Martin

Your code is like your room.

When you have a new room, it's empty, it's pretty neat and clean.

When you start occupying it, things tend to get cluttered here and there…

And a regular cleaning of the room is required.

You could clean your room daily, or weekly or monthly…

But do you clean your code?

Even if you don't clean your room, there can always be someone else who can do it for you,

But when your code is a mess, no one else can clean it better except you.

If people see that your code is a mess, then it's best they start from nothing and build it fast rather than trying to understand it, to clean it and to make it work.

Clean code is readable, easy to understand and it's also easy to make it work if it's not running.

Complex code is hard to read if you don't clean it, only you can understand it and no one else can make it work if it's not running.

Complex code is the code that you write as you are thinking and processing your thoughts on how to solve a problem.

We now have IDEs like VSCode with multiple extensions

Which can help us in cleaning our code, if you are using a framework or language

Then there can be packages that can help you clean your code.

Writing reusable clean code is good

Following best practices and using automated tools to do work is great.

It took me 9 days of coding, 2 days of cleaning and refining my code

So a total of 11 days to get a project running from scratch and ready for deploying and testing in the cloud.

That too I did it only during my free time* and spent 3-4 hours a day working on the features.

*Free time: When I'm not doing anything, I have 100% focus on the code, nothing else matters to me. This was done with writing clean and readable code, focusing on completing one feature at a time. Next I need to think about writing tests…. or will I write them?

26. Computer Lingo #6

Dated: December 2024

I've been building my specifications
and assembling my hardware
The CPU is ready, and my motherboard is in place
I thought I never wanted to assemble or build a PC
But now I'm thinking of building one
The input and output devices have been connected
The system is almost ready,
All I need now is an OS and various software applications
Only my programmer can provide me with a suitable OS
With apps and features that are compatible with my CPU
So that we can both run smoothly

27. March 2022

Dated: 2 March 2022 (written after a farewell gathering on 1 March 2022)

People will come and go
You choose whom you keep in touch
You choose whom you contact
But if you're like me
One who doesn't talk much
And who doesn't even like to contact anyone
I don't even call my parents and friends.
It's going to be like:
If there is any need or something to be done
Then only will I talk or speak or contact people
Which isn't part of the norm or polite thing to do
What we can do is help one another
We are in a place outside of our hometown
We should help each and everyone who comes from where we came from
I may not be able to talk and be polite
Keep in touch with people or be friendly with all.
But I'll give support whenever it is needed
For when I came here I got plenty of help from people around me both the Khasi and Garo friends.

28. What's life like in Williamnagar? – Part #1

Dated: 17 June 2022

Life is quiet and peaceful here as of now in 2022

During holidays there are very few people who come out

While during working days everyone is seen in the DC Office road,

I'm working in the Office of the Deputy Commissioner, Williamnagar, and the majority of the offices are in the same place.

This town is a planned town and it's also a plain area, so once you reach the soil market if you are coming from Songsak or you have reached the junction to the main market if you are coming from Nengkra, you will start seeing one office after the other.

There aren't that many things to do here, basically we have one petrol pump, around four restaurants, three ATM points and the ATM will be very occupied during the first week of each month. On Saturday then I spend time at home, washing and cleaning, sometimes going out to the river to wash clothes. This is the time where I learned to cook, clean and live by myself.

But I am not alone, I'm staying in Nokgil A.we, and in our compound we have many Khasi friends staying, there are also many other Khasi people living in Williamnagar, just in our compound there are around 15 Khasi people, mostly most of them, they go home on the weekends.

Almost every month we would get together and eat together, there will always be some kind of drama, so it's not that boring, and we get to laugh…

The main market is big on Saturdays and this is the day where they also sell furniture products: beds, tables and chairs in the junction before reaching the market, just in front of the MeECL and MTC buildings.

The main transport here are auto rickshaws if you want to get around places, they charge a minimum Rs. 50 from the soil market to the main market.

The weather here is hot: Mid May - Mid September, so a fan is always required.

There are a few Guest Houses and Rent Houses are a bit difficult to get, rent : Rs 5000/month or Rs. 3000/room, and we pay house rent at the beginning of the month.

Right now the timings when most shops close is by 7 PM or 8 PM, normally by 6:30 PM shops start closing down.

Food stalls are mostly made from Bamboo and most of them are temporary.

Fishing is what most men do when they have free time here. Light and Mobile networks most of the time are not that good, it will go out or go down at any time and once rain starts be sure there will be no light during that time, but for me this will do.

There are many other places to visit, and when going out then it's good to wear a cap or carry an umbrella. At home, there are many insects and mosquitoes so it's required to clean the house and your surroundings.

29. Welcome to the Election Branch

Dated: 2022

Welcome to the Election branch

Where everything is urgent and

Everything is sensitive

And you have to do it efficiently

Welcome to the Election branch

Where it's all about working together

And where communication is key

And you need to communicate to get work done

Welcome to the Election branch

Where things are dynamic and

There will always be new instructions

And you have to be updated

Welcome to the Election branch

Where every detail counts

Where you have to be sure of what you do

And you cannot say I think so or I don't know.

So when you are in Election branch

You are giving yourself to this work

You have to commit and work together

Having each other's back and keeping your cool.

30. What's life like in Williamnagar? Part #2

Dated: 31 March 2024

This is what I've noticed with myself

And even my friends have also noticed about themselves

After living in Williamnagar

We find living in Shillong isn't that good after being here.

In Williamnagar:

We don't have traffic jam

There is no rush hour

It's peaceful and quiet

We get good sleep

We sleep well

We eat well

We meet friends

We get together

We play football in the field

We go for picnics

We go swimming

We go fishing

We travel

We relax

We work

The environment and our Khasi Community here is really
where we want to be
We find something that makes us happy
It's a great place to stay
If my grandparents would get the opportunity to come and
stay here
I'd love to take them here.
In a time where I don't have any work to do
This is a good place to relax.
It may not be home for many of us
But it will do.

31. I'd Choose Williamnagar

Dated: 31 August 2024

It's 2024

3 years in Williamnagar,

If I would have to choose between living in Shillong and Williamnagar

I'd choose Williamnagar

It's quiet, I don't have to meet people, and I don't have to spend too much money anywhere.

If I would have to choose between Williamnagar and any other State

I would choose to live in Williamnagar.

Right now it doesn't have proper mobile and broadband connection in the area

No 3-D Google Street View available, no traffic jams, no Swiggy or Rapido or Ubers

No worries

But if I get a different post and I would have to leave Williamnagar

Then It's good, I will leave Williamnagar

But if I'd get to choose to be anywhere I'd choose Williamnagar

Williamnagar is actually the best choice for me right now

No exposure to anything

I will be able to limit myself

I will be able to do what I would like to do and not bother
anyone else

No need to connect with anyone, no need to be in contact
with anyone or anything

32. Friends & Family, Williamnagar

5 November 2024

Shillong is a small place, Williamnagar is even smaller and after being here for 6 months I can see that everyone knows everyone here, it's hard not to find someone with whom you may not have any connections.

When I got the letter (email) that I will be posted in Williamnagar, I wanted to stay there and come home maybe just once or twice a year. I never wanted to come home regularly, and the journey is also a long 6-hour drive from Nongstoin or around 8 hours from Guwahati by small vehicle and almost 12 hours by bus.

It was the first time that I would actually be staying away from home, and since I didn't have any reason to come monthly, and I wanted to stay away from my place, I wanted a hiding place where I could rest and forget the Shillong city life.

Before coming to Williamnagar, I called Barsha D. Arengh, my friend who worked with me in MSSAT earlier, and I got to ask her about Williamnagar, and she helped us book a guest house in House of Mercy to stay for the night when we reached Williamnagar. The first plan when I reached Williamnagar was to stay with Bah Don temporarily until I found a better place to stay, but when I reached Williamnagar, on the same day, Bah Don had to rush home since his mother was hospitalised and in a serious condition, and we didn't get to meet him. I carried many things from home; since I had no place to keep my things, I remembered that there was one officer from the agriculture office who was in Williamnagar, Kong Joplin Lyngdoh. I called her, and she was very generous and kind enough that she allowed me to keep my items at her place for a few days.

The people and the community are close-knit and being part of the Khasi Community in Williamnagar is actually a good thing. Since the location of this place and how Williamnagar is a planned town, it's not hard to see and meet other people after work. Every place is not that far and reachable within 5 km, and provided it is a plain area, commuting with your own vehicle or on foot is very easy.

If you're a Khasi and happen to meet someone from Shillong, once you start talking and getting to know a bit about that person, you will actually find out that there could be someone in Shillong that you both know or are mutual friends. You could even meet past school or college mates, even relatives or friends of relatives whom you've never met or interacted with before in Shillong.

Just from my past experience here, the people I met and the friends I have in Williamnagar, I saw that there is a link to someone I know in Shillong. When I joined in 2021, I got in contact with Bah Donborlang Chyne, who told me to bring football boots when I came here, and since he wasn't there when I joined, he helped me connect to a few friends and I then stayed with Bah Kordorlang L. Kynshi. I met my past classmate, Hubert J. Shullai, where now we got to know each other more than we had in Shillong, and we spent most of the weekend together.

So now, I'd like to write a very short introduction to a few of my present friends and family from Williamnagar. We've got my present roommate Bah Daniel Diengdoh whom David calls my elder brother as he says we look alike. Bah David F. Rapsang, our handsome shakz, Bah Savanth S. Dkhar whom I call Mr. Information as he seems to know and have plenty of information about everything and everyone. There's Bah Shanborlang Warjri, Bah Heubert R. Nengnong, aka the rawon, mister better late than never, Bah Wankit D. Swer aka Ramos, Bah Edmund Suna aka Dr, and Bah Starry Lynser, aka Malit.

When you spend most of the time together, you get to know someone well enough to know exactly what they like and don't like, how they are and what they do.

Since most of the time, I'm with Hubert Shullai aka Garmi, I know that in the evening after coming from work, he will go and play football, after which we will have tea together, and Garmi will take 10 mins to take bath and refresh himself, then we will go shopping, cook and have dinner, and in the morning if there's less soup or daal, he will add more water, heat the soup and add ginger and salt… There are many more people and things to write about but I'm not going to mention them here as it will take too much time.

I made new friends both Khasi and Garo, and in the nok.para where I'm staying, we have become like a family, we eat together, play together, travel together, laugh together, go for picnics and sometimes there will also be conflicts and we get angry with each other. This is all part of the journey, and what's life all about?

If it's not for the ups and downs, highs and lows, ebbs and flows.

33. I ♥? Williamnagar

Dated: December 2024

We were once strangers,

But now I feel so at home with you.

When I come home to Shillong, I long to be with you.

You were unknown to me,

But now I know you, and I ♥? Williamnagar.

When I'm in Williamnagar, I am where I'm supposed to be.

If it's 250 km or more,

It doesn't feel far anymore.

For me, Shillong-Williamnagar feels so near.

The good roads and pleasant weather on the journey,

Doesn't make me tired. The winding roads may make me dizzy,

But knowing I get to see you, I feel better already.

What's there in Williamnagar?

That makes me so in love with Williamnagar.

Is it the weather?

Is it the working environment?

Is it the people and the Garo community out there?

Is it the unity of the Khasi-Jaintia Community in Williamnagar?

Is it the beautiful, quiet and serene nature and environment of Williamnagar?

Is it the peace and quietness of Williamnagar?

Is it the lifestyle out there?

Is it the food out there?

It could be any or all of these things or something that I may have missed mentioning here, that will make you also fall in love with Williamnagar.

I know I ♥? Williamnagar, and so do my friends, and I know they will all agree!

34. Trips

Dated: 15 April 2025
Trips to and from Williamnagar
Ever since coming to Williamnagar
We've covered more km than we did before

Some trips seem very short, while others seem very long
Most trips are smooth, while a few minor accidents do occur
Gladly during all our journeys we reached here safe and sound
There were solo trips and over-crowded trips
Silent journeys and Loud ones also
Every journey is different and has its own twist
There are those who travel home weekly, bi-weekly and monthly

You could take a night bus to and fro Williamnagar
Which takes more than 12 hours to reach, it starts at 4 PM or 5 PM from Williamnagar and reaches Shillong by 6 AM or 7 AM, and if you start from Shillong, the bus moves out at around 6 PM and reaches Rajapara at around 12 AM where it stops for the passengers to have food, and reaches Tura by 4 AM or 5 AM, which then moves out and reaches Williamnagar by 7:30 AM.
You could also take a tourist cab

Which will cut the journey by half the time a bus takes,
From Shillong, they are available from Police Bazar or you can
even contact the drivers, and they normally start the journey
by 6:30 AM and reach by 1:30 PM or later, depending on the
driver and the number of stops they take.
You can also go for a break journey
Make several stops with different means of transport
I once went with Chansam, from Williamnagar to Dudhnoi
on a Winger, then from there we got a Bus to Guwahati,
stayed there and moved to Shillong on another day.
You could even take your own vehicle and take as much time
as you need
If you know the route and drive fast you will reach in 4 hours
30 mins
Normally it takes 5 hours or 5 hours 30 mins only
But you can say that this is a 6 hours journey trip and you can
make two stops in between
And after taking many trips, 5 hours doesn't seem like a long
trip anymore.
The road is smooth, if you go from Assam, it's a very straight
road and if you go from Nongstoin then be ready for some
winding roads from the Nongstoin - Lad Riangdo - Shallang
road.

The part that I like the most about the trips is when I get to
drive
Sitting in the front seat is good, getting to drive is even better

and sitting behind is not a choice I would like to make, so I give props to all my friends who can handle sitting in the backseat with ease.

Taking the bus will be my last resort, I feel it takes too much time, and

I don't get proper sleep, so every time I reach Williamnagar in the morning I feel the need to sleep again the whole day.

35. Ki Kyntien Ai Mynsiem

Dated: 18 April 2025

Ngi kwah ban iohsngew ki kyntien ai mynsiem

Ngi donkam ban ioh mynsiem ban leh ia kano kano ka kam

Lada don mano mano ba ai mynsiem ia phi ba phin leh bha ia kaei kaei, phin ioh mynsiem ban leh bha ia ka.

Kumta hangne ki don katto katne ki kyntien ha ka jingthoh ba lyngkot na ka bynta ki paralok jong nga ha East Garo Hills

Ngi don hangne mynta, bad ha ka por kaba suk ba sain, bad ka iaid ka ieng ruh ka shngain

Ka surok ka bha bad ka jingniah kali ka long kaba suk.

Ka jingleit ka lah ban long kaba jngai bad jrong, hynrei ka jingap bad jingshem ka long kaba sngewtynnad bad kordor.

Phi lah ban kwah ban don ha ïing; phi lah ban kwah ban mih noh na kane ka jaka, bad mano bym kwah ban don ka jingsngew ba phi dei trai ne ban don ha la iing, ha kano kano ka jaka kaba phi don?

Phi don hangne mynta, bad kane ka jaka ka jngai na kaba phi khot ka iing jong phi.

Ka lah ban ym long ha ka jaka kaba phi kwah ban don, hynrei ka long kaba bha tam na ka bynta jong phi mynta.

Ngim ju ioh ia kaei kaei kaba ngi kwah, hynrei ngi ioh thik ia kaei kaei kaba ngi donkam bad U Blei U tip ia kata.

Lehse phi don hangne na ka daw?

Lehse ka dei ka bynta jong phi ban shakri bad ban wanrah jingkylla lane jingbha hangne?

Kumta wat shim ia ka kum ka jingkit kaba khiah, hynrei kum ka jingai kaba la ai ha phi bad pyndonkam bha ia ka.

Ki sngi kiba kham bha kin sa wan, bad ha kawei ka sngi phin sa leit noh na kane ka jaka bad phin sa don sha kano kano ka jaka kaba jan bad la iing lane ha ka jaka kaba phi khot ka iing jong phi, te kiei ki dienjat kiba phin iehnoh shadien?

Hato phin long ka jingshai ne phin long kum ka lyer kaba beh noh bad ym don ba kynmaw?

36. Mitelbea Simsanggre

Dated: 28 April 2025

Thank you, Simsanggre

You've been good to me

You were the first one to take me out of my comfort zone.

You made me a better person than who I was before

Mitelbea, Simsanggre

Na·a angna namako dakaha

Ka·dimeani, dongtoaniko nang·on anga man·chengaha.

Skangna bate na·a angko dingtangataha

You have shown me what life's like,

How to live and adapt to a new environment

How to adjust to new situations and

You've shown me how beautiful you are

Janggi tanganiara maiachim, na·an angna mesokaha,

Songsalo tangna aro gital bakrimpaanirang,

Neng·nikanirangko krae jakrimpae ku·mongpanirang

Nambegipa kamni gunrang, nang'nitoaniko mesokarang

You brought new connections

You help me share new experiences

You took me places where I've not been before and

We spent many amazing moments together

Na·an gital meli-nangrimaniko ra·baaha,

Angna gital u·idapanirangna dakchakaha

Nikronggija, sokrongija rotobegipa biaprangchi angko
rodilarang,

Damsan an·sengbegipa sal somoirangko re·atarang!

I've wanted to visit Garo Hills,

Now I had the opportunity to live here

You are quiet and peaceful, yet you brought people together

I'm grateful to have met you, thank you once again for
everything.

Anga nang·ona songre-songbatna sikbeachim,

Da·o anga ua sal somoirangko chol ra·na man·paaha.

Nang' ka·sinbegipa, tom·tombegipa cholonrang, an·chingko
damsan ong·ataha.

Anga rasong gnange nika, nang' baksa ong·na man·pae,

Mitelbea changsatai nang·ni pilak katchan'gapgipa sal
somoirangna.

37. Ym ju kylla / Ua pangnaba dingtangja

Khasi: Written in 2020

Bakhuid long U Trai
Bakhuid long U Trai
Mynnin, mynta
bad hala karta

Ym ju kylla
Ym ju kylla
Mynnin, mynta
bad hala karta

Ba Khraw long U Trai
Ba Khraw long U Trai
Mynnin, mynta
bad hala karta
Garo: Translated with the help from Luftaansa Bartia Ch
Momin on 2 March 2025

Gitel Rongtala
Gitel Rongtala
Mejal, da·al

Aro jringjrotnan

Ua pangnaba dingtangja
Ua pangnaba dingtangja
Mejal, da·al
Aro jringjrotnan

Dal·gipa Gitel
Dal·gipa Gitel
Mejal, da·al
Aro jringjrotnan

Style of playing:
Verse - Simple Finger Style Picking
Chorus - Rhythm (Down Down Up... Down)
Chords:
Verse:
C Am F G
Bakhuid long U Trai
C Am F G
Bakhuid long U Trai
F M
Mynnin, mynta
C C C
bad hala karta

Chorus:

C

Ym ju kylla

F

Ym ju kylla

G

Mynnin, mynta

C

bad hala karta

38. I have You / Nga don ia Me / Man·e ang' Nangko

Dated: 16 February 2025

English:

I have You

I have You

I have You

With me

I have You

I have You

I have You

Right here

Even when I walk

Even when I sit

Even when I stand

You're there with me

Even when I walk

Even when I sit

Even when I stand

You're here with me

Khasi:
Nga don ia Me
Nga don ia Me
Nga don ia Me
Bad nga
Nga don ia Me
Nga don ia Me
Nga don ia Me
Hangne

Wat haba nga iaid ruh
Wat haba nga shong ruh
Wat haba nga ieng ruh
Me don hangta bad nga
Wat haba nga iaid ruh
Wat haba nga shong ruh
Wat haba nga ieng ruh
Me don hangne bad nga
Garo:
Man·e ang' Nangko
Man·e ang' Nangko
Man·e ang' Nangko
Ang' baksa

Man·e ang' Nangko
Man·e ang' Nangko
Man·e ang' Nangko

Ang' sepango

Ang' rama re·arango

Ang' asongao

Ang' chadengdiko

Na·asan ang' baksa

Ang' rama re·arango

Ang' asongao

Ang' chadengdiko

Na·asan pangnan ang' sepango

Style of playing:

Rhythm (Down Down Up Slap)

Chords:

Em (Down Down Up Slap)

I have You

C

I have You

G

I have You

D

With me

39. In You alone / Ha Me marwei / Nang·osan saksan

Dated: 14 March 2025

English:

In You I find my peace

In You I find (my) rest

In You I find love Lord

In You alone (In You)

In You I am complete

In You I am made new

In You Lord

In You alone

In You I find my strength

In You I find (my) joy

In You I find hope (Lord)

In You alone (In You)

Khasi:

Ha Me nga shem ia ka jingsuk jong nga.

Ha Me nga shem ia ka jingjahthait (jong nga)

Ha Me nga shem jingieit Trai
Ha Me marwei (Ha Me)

Ha Me nga long uba pura
Ha Me la thaw thymmai ia nga
Ha Me Trai
Ha Me Marwei

Ha Me nga shem ia ka bor jong nga
Ha Me nga shem ia ka jingkmen (jong nga)
Ha Me nga shem jingkyrmen
Ha Me marwei (Ha Me)
Garo: 21 May 2025

Nang·osan anga tom·tomako man·a
Nang·osan (ang') neng·takna man·a
Nang·osan Oh! Gitel ka·saako man·a
Ang' saksan Nang·osan (Nang·osan anga)
Nang·osan anga chu·gimik
Nang·osan anga gital ong·aha
Nang·osan Gitel
Ang Nang·osan saksan
Nang·osan anga bil man·a
Nang·osan (ang') kusiniko man·a
Nang·osan anga ka·dongako man·a
Ang' saksan Nang·osan. (Nang·osan anga)

Style of playing:
Rhythm: Down... Up Down Up Down Up Down Up Down

Chords:
Em
In You I find my peace
C
In You I find (my) rest
G
In You I find love Lord
D
In You alone (In You)

Style of Playing:
Rhythm - Down... Up Down Up Down

Chords:
Em C
Nang·osan anga tom·tomako man·a
G D
Nang·osan (ang') neng·takna man·a
Em C
Nang·osan Oh! Gitel ka·saako man·a
G D

Ang' saksan nang·osan (Nang·osan anga)

Em
Nang·osan anga chu·gimik
C
Nang·osan anga gital ong·aha
G
Nang·osan Gitel
D
Ang Nang·kosan saksan

40. It's by Your Love / Dei ka jingieit jong Me / Nang·Ka·saanchisa

Dated: 1 November 2024

It's by Your love I'll be able

By Your love I'll be able

Your love I'll be able

To live

It's by Your love I'll be able

By Your love I'll be able

Your love I'll be able

To wait

It's all about You Lord

It's not about me

It's about Your love Lord

It's for Your glory

It's by Your love I'll be able

By Your love I'll be able

Your love I'll be able

To love

Khasi:

Translated on: 15 April 2025

Dei ka jingieit jong Me ngan lah
Lyngba ka jingieit jong Me ngan lah
Ka jingieit jong Me ka pynlah ia nga
Ban im

Dei ka jingieit jong Me ngan lah
Lyngba ka jingieit jong Me ngan lah
Ka jingieit jong Me ka pynlah ia nga
Ban ap

Ka dei baroh shaphang jong Me Trai
Kam dei re shaphang jong nga
Ka dei shaphang ka jingieit jong Me Trai
Na ka bynta ka burom jong Me

Garo: 29 May 2025
Nang' ka·saachisa anga amsokgen
Nang' ka·sanichi anga amsokgen
Nang' ka·saao anga amsokgen
Jangi tangna
Nang' ka·saachisa anga amsokgen
Nang' ka·sanichi anga amsokgen
Nang' ka·saao anga amsokgen
Sengsona

Pilakan Gitel Nang·ni giminsa

Angni gimin ong·ja

Pilakan Gitel Nang·ni ka.saani giminsa

Nang·ni Rasongnasa

Nang' Ka·saanchisa anga amsokgen

Nang' Ka·saanichisa anga amsokgen

Nang' Ka·saao anga amsokgen

Ka·saskaana

Style of playing:
Rhythm - Down... Up Down Up Down

Chords:
Em
It's by Your love I'll be able
C
By Your love I'll be able
G
Your love I'll be able
D
To live

41. Come to Me / Wan sha Nga / Angona rebabo

Dated: 7 May 2021
Matthew 11:28-30
You say, come, all who are weary,
Come, all who are heavy burdened,
Come to Me all who are weary,
Come to Me all who are heavy burdened
I will give you rest
I will give you rest

You renew our soul
In You there is salvation
You restore our spirit
In You there is perfect peace
Khasi: 2024
Me ong, wan, baroh ki bathait
Wan, baroh ki bakhia jingkit
Wan ha nga baroh ki bathait
Wan ha nga baroh ki bakhia jingkit
Ngan pynsting ia phi
Ngan pynjem ia phi

Me pynthymmai ia ka mynsiem jong ngi

Ha Me don ka jingpynim
Me pynjahthait ia ka mynsiem jong ngi
Ha Me don ka jingsuk ba janai
Garo: 21 May 2025
Na·a agana, re·babo, pilak neng·giparang
Re·babo, pilak baljrimgiparang
Pilak neng·nikgiparang angona re·babo
Pilak baljrimgiparang angona re·babo
Ang' na·simangna neng·takaniko on·gen
Anga na·simangko neng·takatgen
Ching' janggiko na·an gital dakjok
Nang·on ang' janggi jokani.
Chingni gisikko na·a tangchaata
Nang·osan kakket tom·toma.
Outro
Rebabo, pilak gamgiparang
Rebabo, pilak baljrimgiparang
Rebabo, pilak neng·giparang
Rebabo, pilak baljrimgiparang
Ang' na·simangna neng·takaniko on·gen
Anga na·simangko neng·takatgen
Style of playing:
Simple Finger Style Picking
Chords:
C Am
You say, come, all who are weary,
F G

Come, all who are heavy burdened,

C Am

Come to Me all who are weary,

F G

Come to Me all who are heavy burdened

C Am

I will give you rest

F G

I will give you rest

42. Where your heart is / Hangno don ka dohnud jong phi /Jeon nang'gisik ka·tong

Date: 9 November 2024
Matthew 6:2

English:

Do not store up your treasures on this earth that we live in
Where moth and vermin destroy, and where thieves break in
and steal
Where your heart is, that's where your treasure is
Where your heart is, that's where your treasure is
Let your eyes be fixed on things from above
Let your heart be fixed on things that last
Where your heart is, that's where your treasure is
But store up for yourselves treasures in heaven,
Where moths and vermin do not destroy, and
Where thieves do not break in and steal
Where thieves cannot even enter
Khasi:

Wat kynshew ia ka spah hangne ha ka pyrthei ka ba ngi im
Haba ki khniang bad ka sarang ki pynjot ia ka
Bad ki nongtuh ki lah ban tuh ruh.

Hangno ka dohnud jong phi ka don, hangta ka don ka spah
jong phi
Hangno ka dohnud jong phi ka don, hangta ka don ka spah
jong phi
To ai ba ki khmat jong phi kin peit sha kiei kiei kiba na jrong,
bad
To ai ba ka dohnud jong phi kan phai sha kiei kiei kiba neh
Hangno ka dohnud jong phi ka don, hangta ka don ka spah
jong phi

Naba ha ba ka dohnud jong phi ka don, hangta kan don ka
spah jong phi
Naba ha kaba don ka dohnud jong phi, hangta kan don ka
spah jong phi
To ai ba ki khmat jong phi kin peit sha kiei kiei kiba na
shaneng, bad
To ai ba ka dohnud jong phi kan phai sha kiei kiei kiba neh
Hangno ka dohnud jong phi ka don, hangta ka don ka spah
jong phi

Hynrei to kynshew ia ka spah jong phi ha ka hima U Blei
Haba ki khniang bad ka sarang kin ym lah ban bam lane
pynjot

Bad ki nongtuh (ruh) kin ym lah ban rung

Kin ym lah ban tuh ruh

Garo: 22 May 2025

A·gilsako gam-jinko chimongnabe jeon na·a dongenga.

Jeo jo·ong aro maram gimaata, aro jeo cha·ugipa cho·ponge
cha·ugen.

Jeon nang'gisik ka·tong, unon nang' gam-jin ongen

Jeon nang'gisik ka·tong, unon nang' gam-jin ongen

Jekon na·a miksonga, salgisakoni su·songkamgipa ong·china

Jekon   na·a   gisik   ka·tong   on·a   uarang   su·songkame
pangkamgipa ong·china

Jeon nang'gisik ka·tong, unon nang' gam-jin ong·gen.

Indiba Salgio nang' gamchatbegipa gam-jinko chimongbo

Jeo jo·ong aro maram nisiatna man·ja, aro

Jeo cha·ugiparang cha·una man·ja

Jeo cha·ugiparang napna man·ja

Style of playing:

Finger Plucking Style or Rhythm - Down Up Slap Down Slap

Chords

Capo 4: C Am F G

C Am F G

Do not store up your treasures on this earth that we live in

C Am F G

Where moth and vermin destroy, and where thieves break in
and steal

C Am

Where your heart is, that's where your treasure is

F G

Where your heart is, that's where your treasure is

C Am

Let your eyes be fixed on things from above

F G

Let your heart be fixed on things that last

C Am

Where your heart is, that's where your treasure is

F G

43. Na·a Nitobea, Na·a Ka·dingsmiton

Dated: 9 March 2025

You're so beautiful
So beautiful
Beautiful
When you smile

So don't you hide it
Don't you hide your smile
Do not cover it up

Because
You're so beautiful
So beautiful
Beautiful
When you smile
When I look to you
Look to you
Please don't look away

Garo:

Na·a nitobea
Nitobea
Nitobea
Na·a ka·dingsmiton

Ka·sapae donunabe
Donunabe nang' ka·dingsmitako
Pindapnabe ka·dingsimitako

Uni gimin
Na·a nitobea
Nitobea
Nitobea
Na·a ka·dingsmiton
Nang·ko nikon anga
Nang·kon nimanaia
Ka·sapae gipinchiko nie katpanabe

Style of playing:
Rhythm (Down Down Up Slap)

Chords:
C
You're so beautiful
Am
So beautiful

F

Beautiful

G (Down)

When you smile

Notes

December 2024

I know waiting can be different for everyone: how you wait, what you're waiting for, and when your waiting season begins and ends.

What are you waiting for?

When you place high value on what you're waiting for, it is worth the wait.

Why wait?

Wait, because it's all about God's timing.

Inspired by Chris Howland - Under the sun

It's happened before, It'll happen again

Farewells and meetups and family and friends

Seasons of hope and seasons of doubt

Waiting for God, and seeing his works

We dance along, and we live our lives

We keep quiet and we speak our mind

We move along into the dust

It's happened before, It'll happen again

Time marches on, right to the end

There's nothing new under the sun

There's nothing new under the sun

There's nothing new under the sun

There's nothing new

June 2025

The human touch

The flaws we have and mistakes we make

Makes us human!

In a time where everyone is talking about generative AI,

What it can create, and that too in a few seconds or minutes, it lacks the human touch, which can only be appreciated by a few who know how long it takes to make something by hand.

These days, it's a common thing to see that there is an App, a WhatsApp group, a Website, an AI Agent, or a YouTube Channel, for anything you could think of...

When it's overloaded and you have many things at your fingertips, it can sometimes be too much, you could either be drawn towards everything on your phone or want to get away from the device and find something else to do.

People will lie, they may even try to steal or cheat.

These are a few things that come out of the human nature.

Don't do something just to make things happen, if it's going to happen it will happen,

You don't need to go overboard trying to bring something from the ocean into your boat.

Learn to let go, not to worry, to know your limits, to hold onto what you value, and to develop yourself.

Learn to help, to not fear, to know your worth, to hold onto what is right, and to develop relations with others.

Life is not all about getting it right or doing it correctly; we will get things wrong and make mistakes, but we learn from these mistakes, and they give us experiences that make us who we are.

Life is an adventure; it is a journey.
You can either choose to walk alone or walk together.
There will always be times when you will have to climb up a steep hill or go downhill into the valley, and sometimes it could also be like walking in a plain area that's easy to travel in.
Your sailboat can experience smooth sailing or encounter big waves in the ocean; you may even find yourself lost at sea, but that will not be the end; something good is just over the horizon.